THE Monterey Peninsula

Post Card

ESSAGE

THIS ~~FOR AD~~ NLY

PACIFIC GROVE
JUL 16
6 PM
CAL.

CARMEL
JUN 21
8 AM
1911
CAL.

Miss Mattie Q. Yeo

Pacific Cal.

THE Monterey Peninsula

A POSTCARD JOURNEY

Burl Willes

Gibbs Smith, Publisher
Salt Lake City

First Edition

09 08 07 06 05   10 9 8 7 6 5 4 3 2 1

All postcards shown in this book are from the 8,000-card Pat Hathaway Collection of California Views
469 Pacific Street
Monterey, CA 93940
www.caviews.com

Excerpts from *A Wild Coast and Lonely* by Rosalind Sharpe Wall. © 1989 by Rosalind Sharpe Wall. All rights reserved. Reprinted by permission of Wide World Publishing/Tetra, San Carlos, CA, http://wideworldpublishing.com

Published by
Gibbs Smith, Publisher
P.O. Box 667
Layton, UT 84041
Order: 1-800-748-5439
www.gibbs-smith.com

Designed by Kathleen Tandy

Library of Congress Control Number: 2005920119
ISBN 1-58685-783-5

Many people made this endeavor a pleasure and reality. First, I wish to thank independent publisher Gibbs Smith for his enthusiasm and interest in the book and for the help of his fine staff.

I am grateful to Ed Herny, ephemerist and active student of history who introduced me to Pat Hathaway and his remarkable collection of California photographs and postcards. In addition to Pat's kind permission to scan some 350 cards, his knowledge of Monterey history was invaluable.

Archivist Dennis Copeland at Monterey Public Library's California History Room and Denise Sallee, Librarian and Archivist at the Henry Meade Williams Local History Department of Harrison Memorial Library in Carmel, were both extremely helpful. Thank you also to the Pacific Grove Heritage Association and to Todd R. Mocettini for his fount of local knowledge. The late Donald Thomas Clark's *Monterey County Place Names* was an invaluable help; any student of history would find his outstanding research and detective work immensely readable.

Emeritus Professor of Architecture Kenneth H. Cardwell, a Maybeck expert and personal friend of the architect, put to rest the longstanding dispute that Bernard Maybeck was more than a "consultant" at Harrison Memorial Library in Carmel, but indeed the architect of record. Thank you to Rob McNamara for his contribution about the legendary figure Ed Ricketts and to Melinda Pillsbury-Foster for information about her grandfather, postcard publisher Arthur C. Pillsbury.

Thanks to Sheila Huth for her fine job on the book's index. It is always a pleasure to work with fact-checker, editor and proofreader Sayre Van Young. Thank you, Sayre, for your diligent work. Last and certainly not least, my sincere gratitude to Kathleen Tandy who designed the book and jacket, creating original "stamps" for each chapter; she also titled the chapters. I'm sure Kathleen would agree with me that her "sweetie" John L. Hayes deserves recognition for his support throughout the book's creation, his excellent editorial ideas and attention to detail. Thank you so much, Kathleen and John!

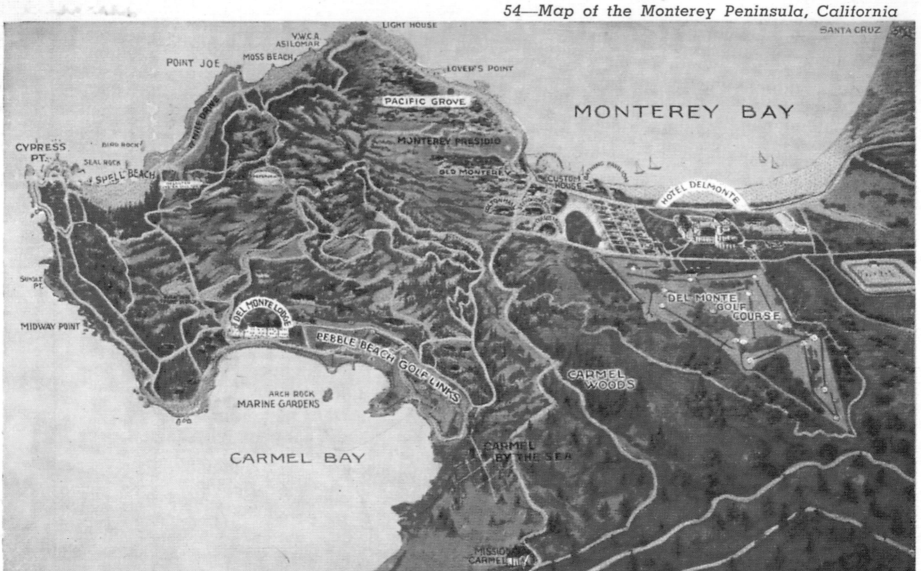

115328-N

Contents

FACING PAGE:
**Map of the Monterey
Peninsula, California.**
B.W. White, no. 54.

Midway Point, 17 mile drive.

Pillsbury Picture Co. No 231

Introduction

Almost mid-way along the California coast, the Monterey Peninsula is a place of unsurpassed beauty. An immensely deep offshore submarine canyon and magnificent kelp beds have created an ecosystem found nowhere else on earth. Sea-borne fogs during the summer provide the extra moisture to sustain the Gowen cypress, the lichen-covered Monterey pines and the twisted Monterey cypress that perch dramatically on rocks along the shore.

Native Americans of the Ohlone tribe were the first to witness the beauty of the area before the founding of Monterey by the Spanish in 1770. Later, Portuguese, Mexicans, Chinese and Japanese settled along the beaches and coves to fish, whale and dive for abalone. Three decades after California statehood was granted in 1850, the grand Hotel Del Monte welcomed the first upscale tourists to the Peninsula in 1880. Travelers made the journey down from San Francisco in just over three and one-half hours on the Del Monte Express, a branch line of the Southern Pacific Railroad. From the hotel there were carriage-ride excursions along a scenic 17-mile route to nearby Pacific Grove, around Point Pinos Lighthouse and into what would later be known as Pebble Beach and Carmel. Some intrepid visitors might travel as far south as the Carmel Mission, *Misión San Carlos Borromeo de Carmelo.*

Early on, commercial photographers captured the Peninsula's scenic charm, and their photographs were sold in the galleries of the Hotel Del Monte. Postcard photographers and publishers found an eager and enthusiastic market for their work. In 1905, photographer Dan Freeman (1876-1962) photographed the schooner *Gipsy* when it ran aground at McAbee Beach, Monterey. He sold $300 worth of postcards in less than a week. His studio on Forest Avenue in Pacific Grove was still operating two years later when Congress passed regulations which permitted "divided backs," allowing the address and message to appear on the same side of the card.

FACING PAGE:
Midway Point, 17 Mile Drive.
Pillsbury Picture Co., no. 231.

This change initiated an explosion in postcard publishing that became known as the "Golden Age of Postcards." Any unusual local event or celebration — a big storm, a shipwreck, the unveiling of a monument — was a postcard opportunity. Prints made one at a time from photographic negatives were known as real-photo postcards. These black-and-white postcards were issued in modest quantities due to the more difficult and expensive production. A real-photo postcard of one's Pacific Grove cottage, for example, might be issued with no more than a dozen copies.

Hand-tinted color postcards, in an era of black-and-white-only photography, were especially popular. They were sent and collected by the thousands.

Today, thanks to the kind permission of collector and Monterey photo historian Pat Hathaway, we are able to reproduce many of these postcards for a nostalgic journey into the history of the Monterey Peninsula and surrounding areas: Carmel, Point Lobos, Big Sur and Tassajara.

FACING PAGE:
Pacifc Grove, Cal.
Publisher unknown.

Pacific Grove, Cal.

3

RIGHT, TOP:
An example of an undivided back.

RIGHT, BOTTOM:
Lover's Point, Pacific Grove, Cal.
An example of a hand-colored postcard.
M. Rieder Publisher, no. 6825.

Lover's Point, Pacific Grove, Cal.

Have you ever seen my summer home? _H ore is view of north end pointing south notice converyhals also green houses with imported fertilizer back of dog also converyance in lover right corner for bright days. *state of thoroughfabo*

Annie Strong

Mrs. Frank Darling
542 Oak
New Monterey
Calfornia.

LEFT, TOP:
A divided back, on the message side of the card below.

LEFT, BOTTOM:
Houses of the 4 Winds, Monterey, Cal.
Real-photo postcard.
J.K. Oliver, photographer, no. 26.

Monterey Bay, MONTEREY, Cal.

On the Waterfront

The name Monterey is composed of the words *monte* and *rey* and literally means "king of the forest." The harbor of Monterey was discovered in 1602, by Admiral Sebastián Vizcaíno, and so named in honor of Count of Monterey, as well as from the neighboring forest of massive pines and other trees.... The forest of Monterey, viewed from the bay, presents the most picturesque appearance imaginable. The surrounding hills of the city, crowned with tall pines and clothed in perpetual verdure, excite in the stranger a feeling at once of surprise and sympathy for the place. The native, as well as the foreign residents, are in constant admiration of it—at least such is the feeling of the writer, whenever he has the honor of being there—his native place. On occasions like those, how fondly he recollects the scenes of his childhood! Those of Monterey, born since the year 1807, to you this sincere sentiment of gratitude is addressed.
　　—Mariano Guadalupe Vallejo, 1850

Although Vallejo credits Vizcaíno with having "discovered" Monterey, the area had been populated with Ohlone peoples for centuries. It wasn't until the arrival of Father Junípero Serra in 1770 that Monterey got its first European settlers. Serra claimed the city for the King of New Spain beneath the same tree under which Vizcaíno had performed divine service over 160 years before. That tree, an important religious symbol for many, was later transplanted to the grounds of the San Carlos Church.

In 1846, Commodore John Drake Sloat sailed into Monterey and raised the Stars and Stripes over the Custom House, declaring the Mexican territory of California the rightful property of the United States. Monterey was already a thriving city, having served as state capital under both the Spanish and Mexican regimes.

FACING PAGE:
Monterey Bay, Monterey, Cal.
Newman Postcard Co.

It was the opening of the Hotel Del Monte in 1880, however, that elevated Monterey from a small, once-important capital to an internationally acclaimed tourist destination. Railroad baron Charles Crocker spared no expense in the construction of his magnificent seaside resort. San Francisco newspapers extolled the "sheltered beach, shady drives, scenery, excellent table, log fires, billiards and ten pins."

The first Fourth of July weekend celebration at the hotel was the social event of the year. Most of the guests arrived on the Del Monte Express from San Francisco where they were met by carriage for the quarter-mile drive to the hotel's main entrance. After a few hours of train riding, guests recovered by taking a leisurely stroll through lush garden paths surrounding the hotel. An elaborate maze of finely trimmed hedges was constructed for just this purpose. Inside, there were warm seawater tanks, divided by a partition into male and female compartments. The ladies would have none of this and made a rush for the male compartment. The quite useless partition was later removed by the obliging hotel staff.

That same weekend there were yachting parties: Harry Tevis in the *Halcyon*, Mervyn and Peter Donahue in the *Nellie*, J.D. Spreckels in the *Lurline*, C.A. Spreckels in *Relief*, and Dr. Merritt in *Casco*. Ballenburg's Band played dance music in the ballroom and "sacred music" on Sunday evening. The "caravansary," as it was called, quickly earned a reputation as one of the "Most Elegant Seaside Establishments in the World."

A fire on April 1, 1887, destroyed the hotel. Although no lives were lost in the blaze, all that remained were the towering fireplaces. The overnight success of the first hotel provided reason enough for another one. In less than a year, a rebuilt Hotel Del Monte welcomed new and returning guests. There was a mile-long racetrack, three polo fields, tennis, archery, croquet, and in 1896, a golf course. After a second fire in 1924, the Hotel Del Monte was rebuilt in a Mediterranean style and was eventually sold to the Navy in 1949.

FACING PAGE:
Main Entrance, Hotel Del Monte, California.
Edward H. Mitchell Co., no. 132.

132 – MAIN ENTRANCE, HOTEL DEL MONTE, CALIFORNIA.

HOTEL DEL MONTE

Stanley and party at Monterey, Cal., March 19th, 1891. Taber, Photo, San Francis[co]

704 — ENTRANCE HOTEL DEL MONTE, MONTEREY COUNTY, CAL., COAST LINE, S. P. R. R.

FACING PAGE:

Hotel Del Monte.
Real-photo postcard.
Pillsbury Picture Co., no. 1817.

LEFT, TOP:

Stanley and party at Monterey, Cal., March 19th, 1891.
Taber, photographer.
Publisher unknown.

LEFT, BOTTOM:

Entrance, Hotel Del Monte, Monterey County, Cal., Coast Line, S.P.R.R.
R.J. Arnold, photographer.
Edward H. Mitchell Co., no. 704.

11

RIGHT, TOP:

The Maze, Hotel Del Monte, California.
Britton and Rey Lithographers, no. 4507.

RIGHT, BOTTOM:

Laguna del Rey, Hotel Del Monte, Del Monte, California.
Edward H. Mitchell Co., no. 618.

THE MAZE, HOTEL DEL MONTE, CALIFORNIA

618 - Laguna del Rey, Hotel Del Monte, Del Monte, California.

LEFT, TOP:

The Roman Plunge, Hotel Del Monte, California.
The Albertype Co.

LEFT, BOTTOM:

Roman Plunge, Del Monte.
Real-photo postcard.
Banfield-Hullinger Co., no. 71186.

ROMAN PLUNGE DEL MONTE. BANFIELD-HULLINGER CO. S.F.   NO.71186

14

4522 Tennis Grounds, Hotel Del Monte, California.

Interior of Del Monte Bath House,
MONTEREY, Cal.

PUBL. BY
PALACE DRUG Co.

FACING PAGE:
Untitled.
Real photo postcard.
Publisher unknown.

LEFT, TOP:
Tennis Grounds, Hotel Del Monte, California.
Britton and Rey Lithographers, no. 4522.

LEFT, BOTTOM:
Interior of Del Monte Bath House, Monterey, Cal.
Palace Drug Co.

564 GOLF LINKS near
DEL MONTE HOTEL, California.

RIGHT, TOP:

Golf Links near Del Monte Hotel, California.
Charles Weidner, photographer.
Publisher unknown, no. 564.

RIGHT, BOTTOM:

Club House and Golf Links, Del Monte.
Banfield-Hullinger Co.,
no. 71168.

FACING PAGE, TOP:

Main Dining Room, Hotel Del Monte, Cal.
The Albertype Co.

FACING PAGE, BOTTOM:

Beautiful California, St. John's Church, Del Monte.
Pacific Novelty Co., no. 3606.

FACING PAGE, FAR RIGHT:

Hotel Del Monte Lobby.
Real-photo postcard.
J.P. Graham, photographer.
Publisher unknown.

CLUB HOUSE & GOLF LINKS, DEL MONTE NO. 71168

HOTEL DEL MONTE LOBBY © 1926 GRAHAM

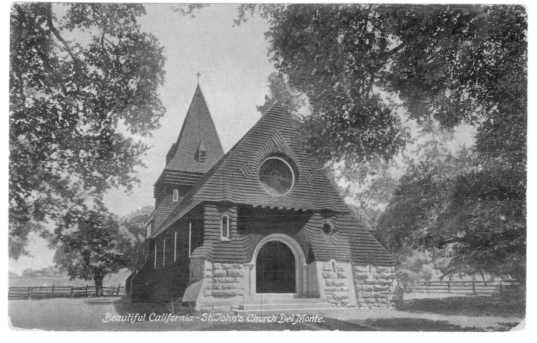

Beautiful California - St. John's Church Del Monte.

CACTUS BED DEL MONTE   P.P.NO. 1254.

18

The grandeur of the Hotel Del Monte and other sites can be seen in the postcards of A.C. Pillsbury. Arthur Clarence Pillsbury (1870-1946), naturalist, inventor and postcard publisher, studied mechanical engineering at Stanford University. While still a student, he designed and built the first panoramic camera. Following graduation, he worked as a photographer for the *San Francisco Examiner*. A month before the San Francisco Earthquake and Fire, he formed his own Pillsbury Picture Company across the Bay, at his Dover Street home in Oakland. Years later, Pillsbury recalled that eventful day, April 18, 1906.

> I grabbed my cameras and started for San Francisco. Fortunately I saved my press badge when I left the Examiner and knowing all the police in the city, I could go everywhere. That Wednesday I covered the entire city making 5 x 7 Graflex views and panoramas of the burning city.
>
> Our house in Oakland was the only place that had running water and dark rooms in those troubled times, and so was soon a busy factory. Salesmen bought material in every city within 500 miles rushing it to us. Others filling orders. A set of pictures and a story was sent to every large paper in the U.S. and abroad.

In 1907, to photograph San Francisco's rebuilding, Pillsbury launched himself in a silk air balloon anchored on a tug in the Bay. After successfully photographing the entire city shoreline, the balloon escaped from the tug and soared 10,000 feet into the air. Fortunately Pillsbury and his aerial photographs survived the unexpected flight and a bumpy landing in the muddy slough of the South Bay.

Soon Pillsbury Picture Company was selling 5,000 postcards a day. Pillsbury again: "I invented a printing machine which enabled a 17-year-old boy who ran it to make 10,000 cards a day hardly getting his hands wet and improving the quality."

"A.C. was a frequent visitor to Monterey and he never left home without his camera," his granddaughter Melinda Pillsbury-Foster told us. "He had many friends on the Monterey Peninsula." Richard J. Arnold (1856-1929), the official photographer of the Hotel Del Monte after 1902, certainly could have been one of them. Pillsbury published postcards of the hotel, buildings of old Monterey and the Peninsula's scenic beauty. Hotel guests might be too busy to write letters, but sending a few Pillsbury postcards really took no time at all.

FACING PAGE:

Cactus Bed, Del Monte.
Real-photo postcard.
Pillsbury Picture Co., no. 1254.

LAGUNA DEL REY DEL MONTE   PILLSBURY'S PICTURES, NO. 1286

THE MAZE DEL MONTE   P.P. NO. 1252

CACTUS BED DEL MONTE   P.P. NO. 1255

De. 12° The Hotel covers acres. My room is
marked with a cross. A lake, crowded with wild birds, is
in front, & the golf links on one side. In the
distance are Monterey & the Bay. L.T.

FACING PAGE, FAR LEFT:

Laguna Del Rey, Del Monte.
Real-photo postcard.
Pillsbury's Pictures, no. 1886.

FACING PAGE, TOP:

The Maze, Del Monte.
Real-photo postcard.
Pillsbury Picture Co., no. 1252.

FACING PAGE, BOTTOM:

Cactus Bed, Del Monte.
Real-photo postcard.
Pillsbury Picture Co., no. 1255.

LEFT, TOP:

Hotel Del Monte.
Real-photo postcard.
Pillsbury Picture Co., no. 1951.

LEFT, BOTTOM:

Del Monte Hotel.
Real-photo postcard.
Pillsbury's Pictures, no. 1889.

Monterey, Cal. from the Old Custom House

22

The carriage ride through the Del Monte Forest, known as the 17-Mile Drive, was designed to acquaint hotel guests with the Peninsula's unique scenery and history. The first mile of the drive passed through Old Monterey where passengers viewed the crumbling remains of the town's rich cultural heritage. The flavor and charm of earlier Spanish days found resonance in the stories and novels of Gertrude Atherton, an aristocratic widow who had lived at Rancho Valparaiso south of San Francisco. Atherton's books were read widely in the U.S. and abroad.

Postcard photographers capitalized on this resurgent interest in Monterey's past and documented buildings as they appeared in the first years of the new century. The series "A Reminder of the Old California Days" was very popular. So, too, were images of buildings that exemplified the "Monterey-style," a blend of Mexican adobe with traditional American wood-porch and balcony. The Larkin House, for example, built in 1834 for an American merchant who later became the U.S. Consul to Mexico in California, was one of the earliest instances of a two-story house in California. Larkin had been influenced by his New England Cape Cod heritage, where the balcony and veranda were common. Postcards extolled other "firsts" as well, such as the "first brick building," the "first frame building" and the "first theatre," but a greater source of enthusiasm was the Old Custom House, the pre-eminent symbol of Old Monterey.

FACING PAGE:

Monterey, Cal. from the Old Custom House.
M. Rieder Publisher, no. 9360.

1778 - Junipero Serra Monument, Monterey, Cal.

2572 - LANDING PLACE OF VISCAINO AND PADRE SERRA, MONTEREY, CALIFORNIA.

JUNE 3d 1770.

728 - San Carlos Church, Monterey, California.

A REMINDER OF THE OLD CALIFORNIA DAYS.

A Reminder of the Old Days.

FACING PAGE, FAR LEFT:

1778 – Junipero Serra Monument, Monterey, Cal.
Edward H. Mitchell Co.

FACING PAGE, TOP:

Landing Place of Viscaino and Padre Serra, Monterey, California.
R.J. Arnold, photographer.
Edward H. Mitchell Co.,
no. 2572.

FACING PAGE, BOTTOM:

San Carlos Church, Monterey, California.
Edward H. Mitchell Co., no. 728.

LEFT, TOP:

A Reminder of the Old California Days.
M. Rieder Publisher,
no. [unreadable]67.

LEFT, BOTTOM:

A Reminder of the Old Days.
M. Rieder Publisher, no. 3618.

The Larkin House, on the corner, built 1835, Monterey, California.
The Albertype Co.

First Frame Building in California, Monterey, Cal.
Newman Postcard Co., no. 19.

60—The First Brick Building in California, Monterey, California

115824

HENRY HOUSE

LEFT, TOP:

The First Brick Building in California, Monterey, California.
B.W. White, no. 60.

LEFT, BOTTOM:

Henry House.
[Family home of First Lady Mrs. Herbert Hoover.]
Real-photo postcard.
Publisher unknown.

9670. A BUSINESS STREET IN MONTEREY, CALIF.

OLD PACIFIC HOUSE 1832 MONTEREY CAL.

MONTEREY, CAL.   First Theatre.   4104

FACING PAGE:

**A Business Street in
Monterey, Calif.**
Detroit Publishing Co., no. 9670.

LEFT, TOP:

**Old Pacific House, 1832,
Monterey, Cal.**
Real-photo postcard, c. 1910.
A.C. Heidrick, photographer.

LEFT, BOTTOM:

**Monterey, Cal.,
First Theatre.**
Paul C. Koeber Co., no. 4104.

2586 — PARADE GROUND AT PRESIDIO, MONTEREY, CALIFORNIA.

LEFT, TOP:

Parade Ground at Presidio, Monterey, California.
Edward H. Mitchell Co., no. 2586.

LEFT, BOTTOM:

Old Custom House, Monterey, California.
Charles Weidner, no. 556.

FACING PAGE:

Monterey, Cal., looking North, showing old custom house on Alvarado St.
Paul C. Koeber Co., no. 4105.

OVERLEAF:

Monterey from the Custom House.
M. Rieder Publisher, no. 4601.

556 Old Custom House, MONTEREY, California.

Monterey, Cal., looking North, showing old custom house on Alvarado St.   4105

Monterey from the Custom House.

Robt. L. Stevenson's House, MONTEREY, Cal.

34

By 1889, Robert Louis Stevenson had become one of the world's most famous authors. Nearly every visitor to Monterey had read, or at least heard of, *The Strange Case of Dr. Jekyll and Mr. Hyde*, *The Silverado Squatters*, *Treasure Island* and *Kidnapped*, but few realized that, a decade earlier, the author had spent a tumultuous time of his life in Monterey. Postcard photographers soon enlightened them.

First, they photographed the building where the as-yet unknown writer probably stayed, the French Hotel on Josepha Street (now Houston). Here Stevenson rented a room on the second floor from the widow Manuela Perez Giardin. Stevenson had come to Monterey to reunite with his love, Fanny Vand de Grift Osbourne, whom he had known in France three years earlier. The only obstacle to the union was that she needed to first divorce her husband. So he waited for her in the adobe building that was later given the name "R. Stevenson House" and was reproduced in many postcards.

Next, photographers found Jules Simoneau. The kind-hearted old Frenchman had befriended the struggling young writer and provided him with a daily meal at his restaurant. When Stevenson fell ill, Simoneau and his wife brought him hot broths and nursed him back to health.

Stevenson postcards were bought with enthusiasm, and many of them found their way into thousands of postcard albums. Meanwhile, the author and his new family — Stevenson was able finally to marry Osbourne in 1880 — had chartered Dr. Merritt's *Casco* to sail to the warm waters of the South Seas, where he built a comfortable home on the island of Samoa. Here he lived, wrote and eventually died, in 1894 at age 44. The Stevenson family library, furniture and memorabilia returned with his widow to San Francisco, and can be seen today at the Robert Louis Stevenson House on Houston Street in Monterey.

FACING PAGE:

Robt. L. Stevenson's House, Monterey, Cal.
Newman Postcard Co., no. 14.

"Robt. L. Stevenson"

No. 25

STEVENSON HOME, MONTEREY.   No. 7/199

FACING PAGE, LEFT:

Robt. L. Stevenson.
Banfield-Hullinger Co., no. 2010.

FACING PAGE, RIGHT:

Stevenson Home, Monterey.
Real-photo postcard.
Banfield-Hullinger Co.,
no. 71199.

LEFT, TOP:

**Jules Simoneau Restrauant
[sic], (1874) Monterey, Calif.**
Real-photo postcard.
C.W.J. Johnson, photographer.
Publisher unknown, no. 2015.

LEFT, BOTTOM:

**Stevenson Home,
Monterey, Cal.**
Real-photo postcard.
Publisher unknown.

#90 DEPOT MONTEREY CAL.. HEIDRICK PHOTO

$\mathcal{A}$nton Charles Heidrick (1876-1955), one of Monterey's premier photographers, came to Monterey as a coronet player with the First U.S. Cavalry stationed at the Presidio. As a civilian, he opened his first photographic studio in 1907. For the next 38 years, A.C. Heidrick rarely missed a postcard opportunity; he was well-known for his panorama views, which brought an additional dimension to postcards and postcard collecting. Heidrick documented everyday life in Monterey, storms that hit the unprotected harbor, unveiling of monuments, life at the Presidio and the burgeoning fishing industry along Ocean View Avenue, later known as Cannery Row.

Fish were plentiful in Monterey Bay, and deep-sea fishing was an added attraction for guests staying at the Hotel Del Monte. By the beginning of the twentieth century, however, out-of-towners were more interested in golf, and fishing was left mostly to the Chinese and Japanese. Salmon brought fish buyers to Monterey, and they began to experiment with the canning of large California sardines. With the arrival of Sicilian fishing star Pietro Ferrante, the sardine industry began to take off. Ferrante introduced local fisherman to the lampara net, a device that had been used for decades in the deeper waters of the Mediterranean and could scoop up substantial groups of fish into massive nets. Sicilian fishermen, familiar with the lampara, were brought to Monterey to work for local sardine canneries. Food shortages during World War I led to a rise in demand. By 1920, Monterey's sardine boom was in full swing.

Life on early Cannery Row was rough and tumble. A mélange of different accents and languages could be heard spoken by the workers, many of them immigrants, hardy enough to survive the grueling labor and long hours. Fishing was conducted at night, under low moonlight, when the iridescent flash of the sardine schools could be observed in the dark waters. The canneries, which employed both men and women, could be just as dangerous as the high seas, because of the exposed equipment, hurried pace and lack of safety regulations.

FACING PAGE:
Depot, Monterey, Cal.
Real-photo postcard.
A.C. Heidrick, photographer,
no. 90.

THE TULIP WAVE OF THE PACIFIC
HEIDRICK Photo MONTEREY CALIF

WRECKAGE ON BOARD
WALK AFTER STORM
4 30 -15-
-3- HEIDRICK PHOTO

HUGE BASKING SHARK -75-
CAUGHT IN MONTEREY BAY, CAL.

UNVEILING OF SLOAT
MONUEMENT MONTEREY
CAL. HEIDRICK PHOTO

FACING PAGE, FAR LEFT:

The Tulip Wave of the Pacific.
Real-photo postcard.
A.C. Heidrick, photographer.

FACING PAGE, TOP:

Wreckage on Board Walk, After Storm, 4-30-15.
Real-photo postcard.
A.C. Heidrick, photographer.

FACING PAGE, BOTTOM:

Untitled.
Real-photo postcard.
A.C. Heidrick, photographer.

LEFT, TOP:

Huge Basking Shark, Caught in Monterey Bay, Cal.
Real-photo postcard.
A.C. Heidrick, photographer.

LEFT, BOTTOM:

Unveiling of Sloat Monuement [sic], Monterey, Cal.
Real-photo postcard.
A.C. Heidrick, photographer.

OVERLEAF:

Monterey Bay, Cal.
[Great White Fleet, 1908.]
Real-photo postcard.
R.J. Arnold, photographer.

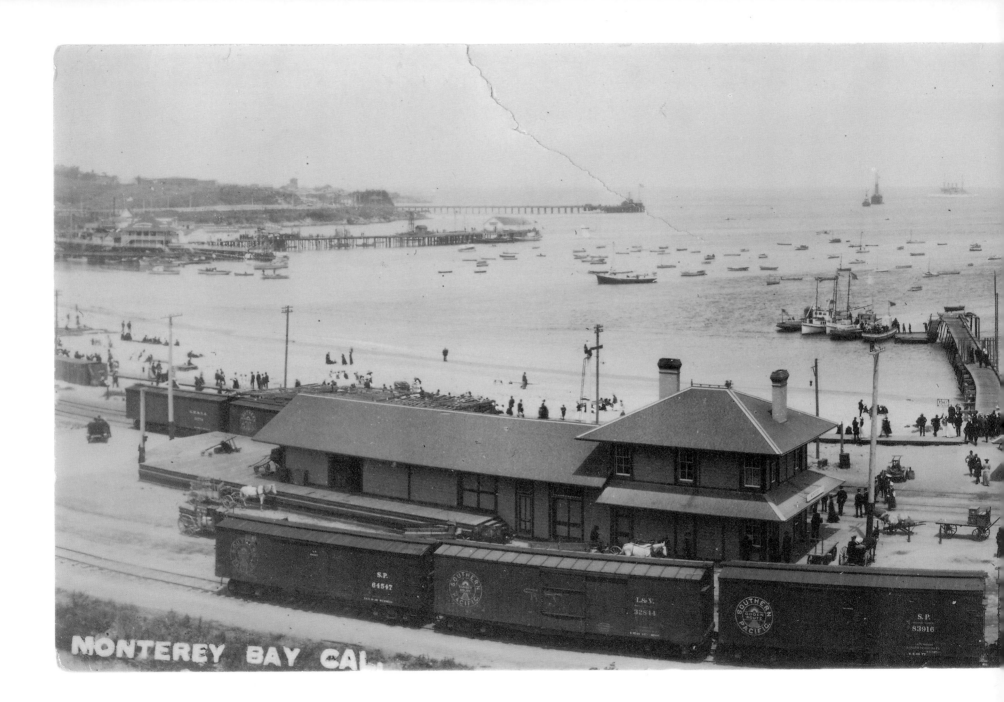

MONTEREY BAY CAL.

Fish Boats, Monterey Bay, Cal.

Salmon Catch, Monterey Bay, Cal.

Beach Scene at Monterey, Cal.

2582 – SALMON CATCH, MONTEREY BAY, MONTEREY, CALIFORNIA.

PRECEDING PAGES:
Fish Boats, Monterey Bay, Cal.
M. Rieder Publisher.

FACING PAGE, LEFT:
Salmon Catch, Monterey Bay, Cal.
M. Rieder Publisher, no. 4616.

FACING PAGE, RIGHT:
Untitled.
Real-photo postcard.
F.C. Swain, photographer.

LEFT, TOP:
Beach Scene at Monterey, Cal.
M. Rieder Publisher, no. 5218.

LEFT, BOTTOM:
Salmon Catch, Monterey Bay, Monterey, California.
Edward H. Mitchell Co., no. 2582.

2727 – Sardine Packing Plant at Monterey, California.

A Small Portion of the Day's Catch for Del Monte Brand California Sardines Pacific Fish Co., Monterey, California

FACING PAGE:

Sardine Packing Plant at Monterey, California.
Edward H. Mitchell Co., no. 2727.

LEFT, TOP:
Untitled.
Real-photo postcard.
Publisher unknown.

LEFT, BOTTOM:
A Small Portion of the Day's Catch for Del Monte Brand California Sardines, Pacific Fish Co., Monterey, California.
Edward H. Mitchell Co., no. 3343.

RIGHT, TOP:
Sardine Cannery, Monterey, Cal.
M. Rieder Publisher, no. 4600.

RIGHT, BOTTOM:
Untitled.
Pacific Novelty Co.

FACING PAGE:
Abalone Shells, Monterey, Calif. Porter Bro's., Pioneer Preparers of Abalone Steaks.
Pacific Novelty Co.

ABALONE SHELLS, MONTEREY, CALIF.

PORTER BRO'S.
PIONEER PREPARERS of
ABALONE STEAKS

MONTEREY, CAL.   Monterey Bay, showing Oil Pier.   4102

52

Ed Ricketts arrived at Pacific Grove in 1923 with the intention of setting up a biological supply business. A handsome and legendarily astute fellow, Ricketts was something of a Renaissance man, delighting in everything from philosophy to classical music to Taoist poetry. While Ricketts was universally admired and respected by local working people, fellow biologists at Stanford University's nearby Hopkins Marine Station considered the college dropout a meddling amateur. Working out of his Cannery Row laboratory, Ricketts had, by 1930, collected the most comprehensive inter-tidal record of the North American west coast in history, and in 1939, published his groundbreaking manual, *Between Pacific Tides*, establishing himself as a leading authority in the field.

In 1930, at a party at Jack Calvin's cottage, Ricketts made the acquaintance of a fellow college dropout and Renaissance man, John Steinbeck. Steinbeck was a local boy, having grown up in the nearby Salinas Valley and dropped out of Stanford University before attaining his degree. With their mutual admiration of the arts and sciences, the two men became fast friends. Ricketts would serve as the model for "Doc" in Steinbeck's novel, the aptly titled *Cannery Row*. In the largely autobiographical work, Steinbeck introduces the reader to the rabble-rousers and street philosophers who called the district home. (It was not until 1953 that the City of Monterey, urged by the success of Steinbeck's book, officially changed the name of the narrow strip from Ocean View Avenue to Cannery Row.) Both men befriended the colorful working-class characters who peopled the streets and local bars. As in Rickett's case, Steinbeck's genius was largely ignored during the time he was there, although with later books such as *Of Mice and Men*, *East of Eden* and *The Grapes of Wrath*, Steinbeck would secure his place among the pantheon of great American writers. He won both a Pulitzer Prize and, eventually, the Nobel Prize for Literature in 1962.

By 1940, Monterey was considered the "Sardine Capital of the World." The 1940 season alone brought in close to $9,000,000 in sardines! After World War II, however, the sardine industry began to decline. Over-fishing had resulted in a drastic shortage of fish off the coast. Many canneries went out of business and were forced to sell their factory equipment to foreign companies in Mexico and South America. A series of fires during the 1950s destroyed many of the remaining canneries.

FACING PAGE:
Monterey, Cal. Monterey Bay, Showing Oil Pier.
Paul C. Koeber Co., no. 4102.

A FISH MARKET
B RETAIL PHONE: 1101

NO PARKING NO PARK

7287

Pier - Monterey, Calif.

POP ERNEST, OPPOSITE CUSTOM HOUSE, MONTEREY, CALIF.

FACING PAGE:

Pier – Monterey, Calif.
[Fisherman's Wharf, c. 1920.]
Real-photo postcard.
Publisher unknown, no. 7287.

LEFT, TOP:

Pop Ernest, Opposite Custom House, Monterey, Calif.
M. Kashower Co., no. 26200.

LEFT, BOTTOM:

Pop Ernest Sea Food Restaurant, Monterey, California.
W.T. Lee Co.

RIGHT, TOP:
Untitled [Monterey Beach
after a Big Storm].
Real-photo postcard.
Publisher unknown, no. 6.

RIGHT, BOTTOM:
Untitled [Captured German
U-Boat, Monterey Harbor].
Real-photo postcard.
A.C. Heidrick, photographer.

FACING PAGE:
Waterfront, Monterey, Cal.
Newman Postcard Co., no. 2.

Waterfront, MONTEREY, Cal.

3938 Light House, Point Pinos. Pacific Grove, Cal.

A View from the Lighthouse

The lonely Point Pinos Lighthouse looked out to sea surrounded by little more than empty beach and sculpted rocks when it was completed in 1854. Little had changed in 1875 when a Methodist Episcopal minister eyed the 100 pine-clad acres a mile to the east, above a grove on the Pacific coast, and envisioned a summer camp. The Pacific Grove Methodist Retreat opened then as just a few makeshift tents, enclosed by a fence to keep out the rowdies from Monterey. Lots sold for $50 each, and soon many makeshift tents were replaced by simple clapboard summer cottages, while grander Victorian houses and commercial establishments were built outside the retreat area.

The Pacific Improvement Company purchased some of the surrounding ranches, but allowed the retreat to "have moral and prudential control over the grounds." Alcohol, tobacco, gambling, foul language, "boisterous behavior" and "immodest bathing apparel" were prohibited.

In 1887, the company opened the El Carmelo Hotel on Lighthouse Avenue, offering reasonably priced rooms facing the ocean on one side and the hotel garden on the other. Guests arriving by train were met at the Pacific Grove station for the short buggy ride to their lodgings. The hotel was a marvel of construction and engineering. Each room was plumbed with Carmel River water and lighted with gas manufactured on the premises. The working hydraulic elevator, still a novelty at the time, was a hit among hotel guests and employees alike. Around 1910, the name was changed from El Carmelo Hotel to Pacific Grove Hotel, to avoid any confusion with the new town of Carmel. It was demolished in 1918; its lumber, however, was recycled for use in the Del Monte Lodge in Pebble Beach.

FACING PAGE:

Light House, Point Pinos, Pacific Grove, Cal.
E.H. Price, photographer.
Paul C. Koeber Co., no. 3938.

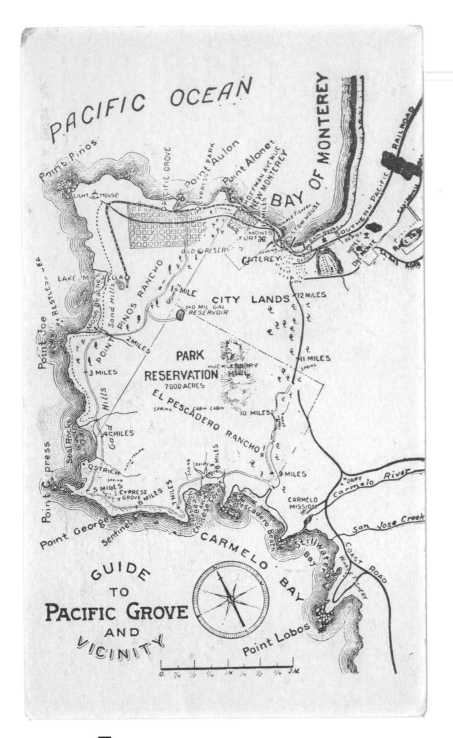

GUIDE
TO
PACIFIC GROVE
AND
VICINITY

PACIFIC OCEAN

BAY OF MONTEREY

CARMELO BAY

Cypress Trees,
Pacific Grove,
Cal.

Pacific Grove from Tea Garden, Cal.

RIGHT, TOP:

Hotel El Carmelo, Pacific Grove, Cal.
M. Rieder Publisher, no. 8132.

RIGHT, BOTTOM:

Pacific Grove Hotel, Pacific Grove, Cal.
M. Rieder Publisher, no. 4596.

FACING PAGE:

Light House Avenue, Pacific Grove, California.
Edward H. Mitchell Co., no. 3045.

3045 – Light House Avenue, Pacific Grove, California.

63

RIGHT, TOP:

Methodist Episcopal Church, Pacific Grove, California.
Edward H. Mitchell Co., no. 3047.

RIGHT, BOTTOM:

Episcopal Church and Rectory, Pacific Grove, Cal.
Richard Behrendt, no. 1306.

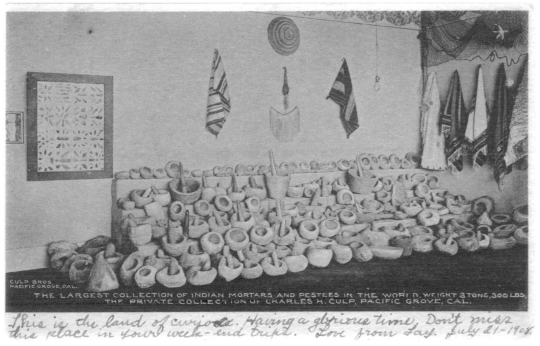

LEFT, TOP:
Untitled.
Real-photo postcard.
Publisher unknown.

LEFT, BOTTOM:
The Largest Collection of Indian Mortars and Pestles in the World....
Culp Bros.

3049 – General View of Pacific Grove, California.

RIGHT, TOP:

General View of Pacific Grove, California.

Edward H. Mitchell Co., no. 3049.

RIGHT, BOTTOM:

Bird's-eye View, Pacific Grove, Cal.

Newman Postcard Co., no. 207.

FACING PAGE:

Street Scene, Pacific Grove, Cal.

M. Rieder Publisher, no. 11831.

Bird's-eye View, PACIFIC-GROVE, Cal.

Street Scene, Pacific Grove, Cal.

Lovers Point, Pacific Grove and Bay, Cal.

Quaint, historic Monterey
City of a byegone day,
Everything that breathes of thee
Makes thee ever dear to me.

COPYRIGHT 1907, M. RIEDER

In 1902, the newly incorporated City of Pacific Grove purchased the promontory, Lovers Point, from the Pacific Improvement Company for a public park. William S. "Bathhouse" Smith, a real-estate magnate and local character, felt the park needed a larger beach, so in a small inlet he packed the rocks with dynamite and made one. Above the beach, Smith built a bathhouse, restaurant and Japanese teahouse. For many years, the Sugano family operated the teahouse, serving tea and small cakes amid paper lanterns, miniature waterfalls and wooden arched bridges.

Near the teahouse, Carroll B. Clark (1868–1951) owned and operated a photography studio above the beach at 17th Street. He had started an earlier tintype gallery in a tent on Forest Avenue in 1895, but this new location facing Lovers Point must have been good for business; many of the untitled and unsigned real-photo postcards of beach-goers at Lovers Point were undoubtedly produced at Clark's studio.

RIGHT, TOP:

**Lover's Point,
Pacific Grove, Cal.**
M. Rieder Publisher, no. 4612.

RIGHT, BOTTOM:

**Pacific Grove from
Lover's Point.**
M. Rieder Publisher, no. 4613.

FACING PAGE, TOP:

**Glass Bottom Boat,
Pacific Grove, Cal.**
M. Rieder Publisher, no. 24312.

FACING PAGE, BOTTOM:

**Bathing Beach with
Japanese Tea Garden at
Pacific Grove, California.**
Charles K. Tuttle Co.

FACING PAGE, FAR RIGHT:

**Japanese Tea Garden,
from Breakwater, Pacific
Grove, California.**
Edward H. Mitchell Co.,
no. 3043.

Lover's Point, Pacific Grove, Cal.

Pacific Grove from Lover's Point. *do you wonder at my taking such a fancy to places like this, ha ha.*

Glass Bottom Boat, Pacific Grove, Cal.

3043 – Japanese Tea Garden, from Breakwater.
Pacific Grove, California.

740 High tide, Pacific Grove, California.

Winter Storm on Bathing Beach.
PACIFIC GROVE, Cal.

2574 — SURF BATHING, PACIFIC GROVE, NEAR MONTEREY, CALIFORNIA.

Greetings from Pacific Grove, Cal.   Bathing in the Surf.

LEFT, TOP:

Greetings from Pacific Grove, Cal.
Bathing in the Surf.
M. Rieder Publisher, no. 637.

LEFT, BOTTOM:

Untitled.
Real-photo postcard.
Publisher unknown.

Light House Avenue. PACIFIC GROVE, Cal.

Hand-colored.

Remembering the celebration that would close the Chautauqua meetings in New York, the Methodists of Pacific Grove, with the aid of the Women's Civic Club, organized their own festival. Thus began the Festival of Lanterns in 1905.

They searched for a theme that would unite the elements of light and water, since New York's Lake Chautauqua was always ringed with lanterns to announce the revival meeting to the community, and found one close to home in the Blue Willow china pattern. The popular pattern illustrated the legend of Kooh-se, the daughter of a wealthy Mandarin, and Chang, her scholarly but impoverished true love. When her father makes plans for Kooh-se to marry a wealthy man of his choosing, she runs away into the night to drown herself. Her father asks the villagers to search for her with lanterns and lighted boats. All that they find are two turtle doves, cooing.

Accordingly, the festival was held on the beach at Lovers Point, and the town streets and waterfront were decorated with 5,000 paper lanterns. The local Chinese fishing community was invited to watch the fireworks, and in time they began to parade in their own illuminated boats on the bay. The lovers were said to be reunited, not as doves, but as monarch butterflies who disappear into the night sky with the promise of return in the fall.

Even today, residents still hang lanterns in their window during the summer festival, and there are fireworks and parades at night.

FACING PAGE:

Light House Avenue.
Pacific Grove, Cal.
Culp Bros.

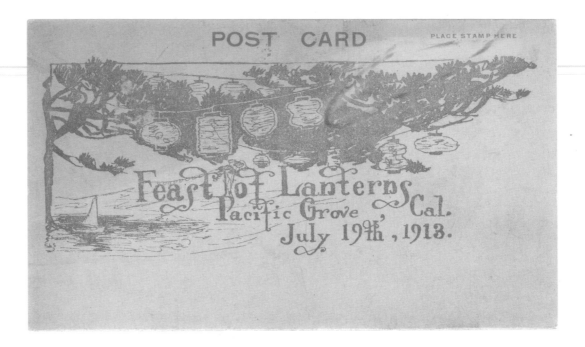

BRANCH OF FAMOUS "BUTTERFLY TREE" PACIFIC GROVE, CAL.

MILLIONS OF BUTTER-FLIES HOVER ABOUT THIS TREE DURING THE WINTER SEASON.

S-462

RIGHT, TOP:
Untitled.
Real-photo postcard.
Publisher unknown.

RIGHT, BOTTOM:
Untitled [Looking up
Forest Avenue].
Publisher unknown.

FACING PAGE:
Untitled.
Real-photo postcard.
Publisher unknown.

9597. CHINESE FISHING VILLAGE, MONTEREY, CALIF.

Less than a mile from Monterey, the largest Chinese fishing village in the Monterey Bay area hugged the shore. Homemade boats called "junks" or "sampans" crowded the shoreline while a single road zigzagged between a jumble of scarlet-curtained shanties on land. From a train window, it could have been an exotic scene along the Yangtze River, the original home for many of the Chinese immigrants. Work in the fishing village was arduous and shared evenly by the men, women and children who called Point Alones home. One either worked on board the fishing boats or on shore, repairing the delicate fishing nets or preparing the day's catch for sale. Red fish, flounder, cod, black bass, shellfish, halibut, mackerel and sardines were caught in abundance. By 1900, 800 pounds of fish were shipped daily to San Francisco. Squid was dried, ground and sent to China where the powder was an important fertilizer in the rice fields. Abalone shells, a popular mantle-piece souvenir, were sold to tourists.

Once a year, the unrelenting work schedule was put on hold for the Chinese New Year celebration. Finely decorated paper dragons danced down the beach amid costumed crowds and bursting firecrackers. Curious townspeople joined the festivities, for all were welcome. But few tourists ventured inside the actual village—the smell of drying squid on some days was said to be quite offensive.

Fortunately, the oceanfront village had been appreciated by postcard photographers, because soon it was gone. In 1905, after a load of rotten squid washed back to shore at Lovers Point, the village was ordered to close. The Chinese refused. A year later, when the Chinese again refused to leave, a suspicious fire broke out, and the village was destroyed.

RIGHT, TOP:

**Chinese Fishing Village,
New Monterey, Cal.**
Newman Postcard Co.

RIGHT, BOTTOM:

**Chinese Fishing Village,
Monterey Bay, California.**
Edward H. Mitchell Co.

Chinese Fishing Village
New Monterey, Cal.

CHINESE FISHING VILLAGE, MONTEREY BAY, CALIFORNIA

Chinatown, Pacific Grove, Cal.

Chinatown, Pacific Grove, Cal.

LEFT, TOP:

Chinatown, Pacific Grove, Cal.

M. Rieder Publisher, no. 4611.

LEFT, BOTTOM:

Chinatown, Pacific Grove, Cal.

M. Rieder Publisher, no. 4599.

Chapel Window, Asilomar

A14

The Young Women's Christian Association (YWCA), seeking a calm, resplendent place to hold its annual conferences, was enchanted with the seacoast beyond Point Pinos. Thirty acres were offered to them by the Pacific Improvement Company for the 1913 conference. The YWCA decided to keep the property, and a contest was given to name it; Miss Helen Salisbury won with her name, "Asilomar," based on the Spanish words *asilo* (refuge) and *mar* (sea).

With its fragrant pines and virgin sand dunes, Asilomar would provide the ideal place for both calm meditation and important discussion. Phoebe Hearst, an early backer of the project, brought in architect Julia Morgan, of Hearst Castle fame, to design the buildings. Morgan used local materials (redwood from Big Sur, stones from Pebble Beach) to create sixteen magnificent buildings in the arts and crafts style. Construction at Asilomar (1913-1928) attracted the serious and the merely curious. Postcards offer glimpses of construction as well as the first years in operation.

In 1956, the property, by then grown to 60 acres, was sold (for a fraction of its value) to the State of California on the condition that it become a state park. Thirteen of the original sixteen buildings remain and were designated a National Historic Landmark in 1987.

FACING PAGE:

Chapel Window, Asilomar.
Real-photo postcard.
Publisher unknown, no. A14.

RIGHT, TOP:
**Assembly Hall, YWCA,
Asilomar, Cal.**
Edward H. Mitchell Co., no. 2798.

RIGHT, BOTTOM:
Untitled [Asilomar front drive
under construction, 1913].
Publisher unknown.

Tent Houses, Y.W.C.A. Conference Grounds, Asilomar, Cal

740 Lounge, Asilomar.

LEFT, TOP:

**Tent Houses, Y.W.C.A.
Conference Grounds,
Asilomar, Cal.**
Pacific Novelty Co., no. 2799.

LEFT, BOTTOM:

Lounge, Asilomar.
Real-photo postcard.
Publisher unknown, no. 740.

RIGHT, TOP:

Asilomar, Cal., 1914.
Real-photo postcard.
A.C. Heidrick, photographer.

RIGHT, BOTTOM:

Coast at Asilomar.
Pillsbury Picture Co., no. 7879.

FACING PAGE:

Asilomar.
Real-photo postcard.
Publisher unknown, no. 6682.

ASILOMAR

6682

TANKER F.H. BUCK ON ROCKS AT PT PINOS
MONTEREY BAY 5-4-24 HEIDRICH PHOTO

92

Real-photo postcards documented any event that brought out the crowds. Faulty navigation was said to be the cause of the shipwreck of the *Frank H. Buck* off Point Pinos in 1924. Traveling at "full speed ahead," the vessel slid over two shallow reefs before coming to an abrupt halt atop the jagged rocky shore. A commercial liner traveling from San Francisco to Monterey, the ship was carrying 39 passengers at the time of the wreck. Anton Charles Heidrick (1876-1955), one of Monterey's most talented photographers, was soon on the scene with his camera. Fortunately there were no casualties, and Heidrick photographed the ingenious rescue by use of the "Breeche's Buoy," a device used to unload the passengers. A rope line was extended from the ship's deck to the beach, offering an undoubtedly speedy and exciting ride to safety.

FACING PAGE:

Tanker F.H. Buck on Rocks at Pt. Pinos, Monterey Bay 3-4-24.
Real-photo postcard.
A.C. Heidrick, photographer, no. 2.

RIGHT, TOP:
Untitled.
Real-photo postcard.
A.C. Heidrick, photographer.

RIGHT, BOTTOM:
Untitled.
Real-photo postcard.
A.C. Heidrick, photographer.

FACING PAGE:
SS Frank H. Buck, near Point Pinos.
Real-photo postcard.
A.C. Heidrick, photographer.

2590 – "THE OSTRICH", SEVENTEEN MILE DRIVE, NEAR MONTEREY, CALIFORNIA.
ON LINE OF S. P. R. R.

The Green and the Blue

The 17-Mile Drive was established in 1881 for guests at the Hotel Del Monte. Until the first motorcars arrived, the trip was made by horse-drawn carriage through Pacific Grove, along the coastline into the forest of Pebble Beach, out the Carmel Hill gate and back to Monterey, a journey of approximately seventeen miles. It soon became known as the most delightful and picturesque drive in America. An early visitor to the Hotel Del Monte and the Peninsula was New York banker Jay Pierpont Morgan. His praise for the area was well-received by the press. "I have enjoyed all that the Cote d'Azur on the French Riviera could offer, but it can not begin to compare with the beauty to be found on the Monterey Peninsula." Postcard photographers were just as enthusiastic, and every bend in the 17-Mile Drive was a scenic opportunity.

The "Ostrich Tree," created by the combined growth of two wind-swept Monterey cypresses, was a popular postcard that sold well even after the tree was destroyed by a storm in 1916. The cypress drive meandered along the coast, past the "Lone Cypress Tree," around Pescadero Point and into the small protected bay with its pebbled beach. Known originally as Pescadero for the Chinese fishing village located here from 1868 through 1912, its name was changed to Pebble Beach around 1907 when Charles Crocker and the Pacific Improvement Company started to develop the area as a summer resort.

FACING PAGE:
"The Ostrich", Seventeen Mile Drive, Near Monterey, California, on Line of S.P.R.R. Edward H. Mitchell Co., no. 2590.

Entrance . 17. Mile Drive Pacific Grove, Calif.

106 Stinson

35 Mile Auto Boulevard, Pacific Grove, California

Forest Lodge 17 Mile Drive, Pacific Grove, Cal.

FACING PAGE:

Entrance, 17 Mile Drive, Pacific Grove, Calif.
Real-photo postcard.
Stinson, photographer, no. 106.

LEFT, TOP:

35 Mile Auto Boulevard [sic], Pacific Grove, California.
Edward H. Mitchell Co., no. 3040.

LEFT, BOTTOM:

Forest Lodge, 17 Mile Drive, Pacific Grove, Cal.
M. Rieder Publisher, no. 11829.

RIGHT, TOP:

**Lone Cypress Point,
Scenic Seventeen Mile
Drive, Monterey Peninsula,
California.**
California Parlor Tours Co.

RIGHT, BOTTOM:

"The Loop," 17 Mile Drive.
Western Card Co., no. 4538.

LONE CYPRESS POINT, SCENIC SEVENTEEN MILE DRIVE, MONTEREY PENINSULA, CALIFORNIA

"THE LOOP" 17 MILE DRIVE.   4538

The Loop on the 17 Mile Drive, near Pacific Grove, Cal.

2580 — ROAD THROUGH CYPRESS GROVE, SEVENTEEN MILE DRIVE, NEAR MONTEREY CALIFORNIA.   ON LINE OF

LEFT, TOP:

The Loop on the 17 Mile Drive, near Pacific Grove, Cal. M. Rieder Publisher, no. 6824.

LEFT, BOTTOM:

Road Through Cypress Grove, Seventeen Mile Drive, near Monterey, California. On Line of the Southern Pacific. Edward H. Mitchell Co., no. 2580.

OVERLEAF:

Midway Point, 17 Mile Drive, near Pacific Grove, Cal. M. Rieder Publisher, no. 8089.

Drive, near Pacific Grove, Cal.

RIGHT, TOP:

Seal Rocks from 17-Mile Drive, California.
Bell Magazine Agency, no. M29.

RIGHT, BOTTOM:

Untitled [View towards Pt. Lobos from Pebble Beach, 1917].
Real-photo postcard.
Leopold Hugo, photographer.
Publisher unknown.

1405:—Sand Dunes on the 17 Mile Drive, Monterey Peninsula, Calif.

23622

LEFT, TOP:

Sand Dunes on the 17 Mile Drive, Monterey Peninsula, Calif.
Publisher unknown, no. 1405.

LEFT, BOTTOM:

Sand Dunes on the 17 Mile Drive.
Hotel Del Monte.

**A Scene Near Cypress Point –
17 Mile Drive.**
Edward H. Mitchell Co., no. 4539.

**Cypress Trees on Seventeen
Mile Drive, Monterey,
California.**
Detroit Publishing Co., no. 71687.

761   Lodge at Pebble Beach, 17 Mile Drive, Monterey Co. Cal.

To attract wealthy prospective residents to Pebble Beach, a picturesque wood-and-stone lodge was built by the Pacific Improvement Company and opened in 1909. Set back from the sea, while maintaining a splendid vista of the coast as far as Point Lobos, the Pebble Beach Lodge blended harmoniously with the surrounding forest and was a favorite stopping-off point along the 17-Mile Drive. A few years after opening, a row of cottages was added, and the lodge became known as Del Monte Lodge; after more remodeling and additions, the name was changed again to the Lodge at Pebble Beach.

Samuel F. B. Morse, who envisioned open space along the ocean, spearheaded the sensitive development that preserved the natural beauty of Pebble Beach. When the Pebble Beach Lodge was destroyed by fire in 1917, Morse built another lodge on the site. The new lodge and the spectacular oceanfront Pebble Beach Golf Links opened in 1919. The new golf links were an immediate success, and postcards were soon available for visitors and collectors. As part of the second phase of the successful resort development, the Monterey Peninsula Country Club opened its Dunes Course in 1926. Few golfers to Pebble Beach returned home without first sending a postcard.

FACING PAGE:

Lodge at Pebble Beach, 17 Mile Drive, Monterey Co., Cal. Edward H. Mitchell Co., no. 761.

Fireplace in Great Hall, Pebble Beach Lodge, California

Dining Room, Pebble Beach Lodge, Monterey Co., Cal.

71575 PERGOLA, PEBBLE BEACH LODGE, ON THE SEVENTEEN MILE DRIVE, MONTEREY, CALIFORNIA

FACING PAGE, FAR LEFT:

Fireplace in Great Hall, Pebble Beach Lodge, California.
Publisher unknown.

FACING PAGE, TOP:

Fireplace in Great Hall, Pebble Beach Lodge, Pebble Beach, Monterey County, California.
Publisher unknown.

FACING PAGE, BOTTOM:

Dining Room, Pebble Beach Lodge, Monterey Co., Cal.
Real-photo postcard.
Publisher unknown.

LEFT, TOP:

Pergola, Pebble Beach Lodge, on the Seventeen Mile Drive, Monterey, California.
Publisher unknown, no. 71575.

LEFT, BOTTOM:

Untitled.
Real-photo postcard.
Publisher unknown.

DEL MONTE LODGE

7922

The Lodge, Pebble Beach, 17 Mile Drive, Monterey Co., Calif.

4715

FACING PAGE:

Del Monte Lodge.
Publisher unknown, no. 7922.

LEFT, TOP:

**The Lodge, Pebble Beach,
17 Mile Drive, Monterey Co.,
Calif.**
Pacific Novelty Co., no. 4715.

LEFT, BOTTOM:

**Beach Club and Stillwater
Cove, Del Monte Lodge,
Pebble Beach, California.**
The Albertype Co.

GOLF LINKS – PEBBLE BEACH   DEL MONTE, CALIFORNIA

RIGHT, TOP:

Beach Bath House,
Monterey Peninsula
Country Club.
The Albertype Co.

RIGHT, BOTTOM:

Monterey Peninsula
Country Club, California.
The Albertype Co.

FACING PAGE:

11th Hole at Pebble Beach.
Real-photo postcard.
Publisher unknown.

11th Hole at Pebble Beach.

117

Carmel Mission and Valley, Carmel By The Sea, California.

Bohemians in the Mist

The mission that Father Junípero Serra established inside the Presidio at Monterey in 1770 was moved a year later to a more fertile site near the Carmel River. Here, in its present location, it was renamed *Misión San Carlos Borromeo del Río Carmelo*. A century later, in 1882, under the rubble of the collapsed roof and sandstone walls, four stone slabs were uncovered. Historians were consulted, and it was announced that Father Serra must be buried beneath one of these slabs.

On July 3, 1882, a notice was posted on the bulletin board of the Hotel Del Monte in Monterey.

The remains of Padre Junípero Serra and three others will be disinterred today at the old Carmel Mission at three P.M. sharp. The San Francisco St. Patrick Cadets and the Third Regimental Band will be in attendance and the guests of the Hotel Del Monte are cordially invited to be present.

A colorful group with their "conveyances" gathered for the simple, impressive ceremony. "Six-in-hands, four-in-hands, teams with liveried attendants, buggies, hay wagons, carts; swells of both sexes in fashionable riding-habit, vaqueros on mustangs, and Indians on mules," reported an eyewitness for the *San Francisco Argonaut*.

Minimum restoration soon followed, but it was not until much later that the building's historic architectural integrity was given proper attention. Joseph Jacinta "Jo" Mora received the commission to design and build the Father Serra sarcophagus. Mora, a multitalented artist, moved to Carmel in 1923 to be near his Carmel Mission work, and the magnificent bronze and travertine marble monument was unveiled on October 12, 1924.

FACING PAGE:
Carmel Mission and Valley,
Carmel By The Sea, California.
S. L. & Co., No. E12206.

RIGHT, TOP:

Carmel Mission Valley.
Pillsbury Picture Co., no. 220.

RIGHT, BOTTOM:

**Carmelo Mission,
Monterey County, Cal.,
Founded in 1774.**
M. Rieder Publisher, no. 2836.

FACING PAGE, TOP:

**Interior Carmel Mission,
near Pacific Grove, Cal.**
Paul C. Koeber Co., no. 3925.

FACING PAGE, BOTTOM:

Carmel Mission.
Pillsbury Picture Co., no.128.

FACING PAGE, FAR RIGHT:

**The Escalero, Carmel
Mission, Monterey, Cal.**
M. Rieder Publisher, no. 7781.

Carmel Mission Valley.   Pillsbury Picture Co. No. 220

Carmelo Mission, Monterey County, Cal.
Founded in 1774.

Interior Carmel
Mission, near
Pacific Grove Cal.

3925

The Escalero, Carmel Mission,
Monterey, Cal.

CARMEL MISSION.

© P.P. No.13.8H.

CARMEL VALLEY

MA 80 LAWS

Pine Inn, John B. Jordan, Prop.
Carmel-by-the-Sea.

Pho. L. S. Slevin.

124

ouis S. Slevin (1878-1945) moved to Carmel in 1903 and opened the first post office in his shop on Ocean Avenue. For nearly four decades, he photographed Carmel and Big Sur and the Monterey Peninsula. His real-photo postcards portray vivid images of everyday life in early Carmel. Writing in the January 19, 1945, issue of the *Carmel Pine Cone*, Slevin recalled his first visit to Carmel-by-the-Sea:

There was a hotel before the Carmel-by-the-Sea regime. That was the Hotel Carmelo, located on the corner of Junipero Street and Ocean Avenue. It resembled an ordinary two-story house. In 1903 the building was moved down Ocean Avenue and set between Lincoln and Monte Verde Streets. Additions were made to it and it became the Pine Inn.

In order to accommodate the overflow of the Pine Inn of 1903, which had very limited accommodations, a row of tents extended up to Lincoln Street. I was here for a vacation and occupied one of the tents. I ate my dinners at Pine Inn and was allowed the special rate of 40 cents for poor people.

Later that year, Slevin decided to move to Carmel and bought a lot on Ocean Avenue from James F. Devendorf, the resident representative of the recently formed Carmel Development Company. Devendorf and his partner Frank H. Powers, new owners of Carmel City, renamed it City of Carmel-by-the-Sea. Hoping to create an artistic community, they offered lots cheaply to artists and writers.

Slevin continues:

J.F. Devendorf was very active in promoting the sale of lots, flying around with his horse and buggy through the bushes and over logs at an amazing rate. No high powered sales tactics were used. The person had to have the desire to purchase a lot, and Mr. Devendorf would simply aid him to select one.

He was most solicitous for the comfort of those who located here and was called upon to attend to all sorts of commissions from getting a tube of burnt sienna for Miss E. Chandler to assisting one of the Murphys across Ocean Ave. when it was like a river during a downpour. He also provided water for the people when the pump broke down. He was called the father of Carmel.

S levin cleared his lot on Ocean Avenue and built one of the first stores in Carmel. His sign above the door announced for sale abalone jewelry, stationery, fishing tackle, Kodak film processing and postcards. Inside the store, a post office opened in March 1904 where Slevin served as postmaster. The incidental tasks of a 1904-1915 postmaster were much more varied than the present ones, as Slevin recalled in the *Carmel Pine Cone*, January 19, 1945:

Strangers knew of no one else to call on for their needs, so besides receiving numerous requests for information about the weather, prices of lots, how far away is the Mission, etc. etc., I had a request from Miss Dickerson of Providence, R.I. for several specimens of toads and frogs native to this region. There happen to be two varieties of toads and two or three frogs. This commission was not so easy to accomplish, but specimens of all were gradually sent, marked "keep cool" or "keep warm" according to season.

Another request was from the late Prof. Geo. Davidson of San Francisco. He wanted to know the elevations of the highest hills in the vicinity. He sent a barometer, and with my brother, J.R. Slevin, I tramped to the hill tops, and took the elevations.

COPYRIGHT 1907
BY L.S. SLEVIN
CARMEL, CAL.

CARMEL BEACH AND BATH HOUSE, CARMEL, CAL.

RIGHT, TOP:

Carmel by the Sea.
Publisher unknown.

RIGHT, BOTTOM:

Pine Inn, Carmel, Cal.
L.S. Slevin, photographer.

LEFT, TOP:

Pine Inn Cottages, John B. Jordan Prop., Carmel by the Sea, California.
The Albertype Co.

LEFT, BOTTOM:

Hotel La Playa, The Strand, Carmel-by-the-Sea, California.
L.S. Slevin, photographer.
Carmel-by-the-Sea Pharmacy.

George Sterling, a well-connected poet and member of San Francisco's Bohemian Club, moved to Carmel in 1906. Sterling was followed by many of his friends. Some, like Jack London and Ambrose Bierce, just visited. But others bought lots from Devendorf and stayed. For these artists and many early Carmel residents, days were devoted to artistic creation while nights were given to beach parties where guests feasted on abalone, drank wine and sang songs—the most famous being the "Abalone Song," a rollicking drinking song whose verses attributed to Sterling include the following:

Oh some drink rain and some champagne,
And whiskey by the pony
But I will try a dash of rye
And a hunk of abalone.

I telegraph my better half
By Morse or by Marconi
But when in need of greater speed
I send an abalone.

He wanders free beside the sea,
Wher'er the coast is stony.
He flaps his wings and madly sings,
The plaintive abalone.

In a more serious vein, the Forest Theatre, an open-air theatre built amidst the pine trees, produced its first play, *David,* in 1910. Aided by their candle lamps, local residents walked there, sat on benches between pine trees and watched locally written plays. Some of the productions were the subject of real-photo postcards. The success of the Forest Theatre led to the opening of the Golden Bough, a community theatre that became known as one of the finest in the nation.

FACING PAGE:

Carmel Bay, California.
The Albertype Co.

RIGHT, TOP:

Entrance to Forest Theatre, Carmel-by-the-Sea, Calif.
Real-photo postcard.
Publisher unknown.

RIGHT, BOTTOM:

Untitled [Forest Theatre].
Real-photo postcard.
Publisher unknown.

FACING PAGE:

Forest Theatre, Carmel, Cal.
Real-photo postcard.
L.S. Slevin, photographer.

COPYRIGHT 1912.
L. S. SLEVIN.
FOREST THEATRE,
CARMEL, CAL.

PHOTO BY L.S. SLEVIN

FACING PAGE, LEFT:

Carmel by the Sea Historical Pageant.
[Forest Play of 1911.]
L.S. Slevin, photographer.

FACING PAGE, RIGHT:

Carmel by the Sea Historical Pageant.
[Forest Play of 1911.]
L.S. Slevin, photographer.

LEFT, TOP:

Untitled.
Real-photo postcard.
Publisher unknown.

LEFT, BOTTOM:

Court of the Golden Bough, Carmel, California.
L.S. Slevin, photographer.
The Albertype Co.

Home of Robinson Jeffers the Poet
Carmel by the Sea, Calif.

ZS 382

Most of the original bohemians were gone by 1914, but they had brought national attention to their lifestyle and the beauty of Carmel's natural setting. In 1914, encouraged by enthusiastic letters from George Sterling, Una and Robinson Jeffers bought a knoll above the beach on Ocean View Avenue. Soon Jeffers began to build Tor House, inspired by a Tudor barn he and Una Jeffers had seen in England. Most of the work he did himself, hauling up stones from the beach below; the cottage was completed by 1919 and Hawk Tower, a play area for his twin boys, in 1924. The unusual dwelling, subject of numerous postcards, was an ongoing project that lasted for decades. Here the poet lived with his family and wrote about the wild coast he loved.

The building project inspired a creative quickening, and his 1924 *Tamar and Other Poems* established his reputation. His poems reflected a philosophy that Jeffers called Inhumanism, and expressed his belief that mankind had become destructive and self-absorbed, ignoring the natural world.

>…the greatest beauty is
>Organic wholeness, the wholeness of life and things, the divine beauty
>of the universe. Love that, not man
>Apart from that…

Medea, his 1946 adaptation of the Euripides classic, was written for actress Judith Anderson, and brought him international acclaim. Robinson Jeffers died at Tor House in 1962 at age 75.

FACING PAGE:

Home of Robinson Jeffers, the Poet, Carmel by the Sea, Calif.
Zan of Tamalpais, no. 382.

C. More Curtis, Carmel, Cal.

4178

The years from 1903 until 1922 were the days of milk shrines, the Community Bulletin Board, dusty roads in the summer and gullies filled with cut branches in the winter. Each neighborhood had its milk shrine where residents left their change at night, and every morning Mr. Waterbury would drive up with his horse and wagon and leave the milk bottles in the proper section. "The Bulletin Board on Ocean Avenue near Lincoln ran until about 1923," L.S. Slevin recalled. "Articles found were hung on it. A picture shows two shoes (not mates), a pair of specs, a key and numerous notices."

In 1922, Ocean Avenue was paved. Slevin continues, "Before that it was a dusty road full of holes, ruts and gullies. The principal bumps were known by name—'Devil's Staircase,' the 'Witch's Caldron,' the 'Hinges of Hades' and others."

A noted local personality was Delos Curtis. He came to Carmel around 1908 and found work in the business owned by Catherine More; they later married and together ran a restaurant/ice cream shop/candy kitchen on Ocean Avenue that became the center of local activity. In the early days, he ran the bath house at the beach, showed movies in the Manzanita theater and invented delicate new flavors of ice cream. He was a generous spirit, bringing trays of food to those too poor or too sick to come to his restaurant. He also sponsored an annual Christmas party with gifts, as well as his candy canes, for each child, until the town's population swelled and he could no longer afford it. His death in 1937 was noted with the closing of most Carmel businesses for his funeral.

FACING PAGE:

C. More Curtis, Carmel, Cal.
Pacific Novelty Co., no. 4178.

Untitled.
Real-photo postcard.
L.S. Slevin, photographer.

**Bulletin Board, Carmel,
California.**
Real-photo postcard.
L.S. Slevin, photographer.

THE DAILY BREAD

FAR LEFT:
Milk Shrine, Carmel, California, 1927.
L.S. Slevin, photographer.

LEFT:
The Daily Bread.
Real-photo postcard.
Publisher unknown.

FACING PAGE, FAR LEFT:
Untitled [Delos Curtis].
Real-photo postcard.
L.S. Slevin, photographer.

FACING PAGE, TOP:
Miss Calherton and Miss Johnson at Carmel, 1908.
Real-photo postcard.
Publisher unknown.

FACING PAGE, BOTTOM:
Untitled.
Real-photo postcard.
L.S. Slevin, photographer.

LEFT, TOP:
Untitled.
Real-photo postcard.
Publisher unknown.

LEFT, BOTTOM:
Untitled.
Real-photo postcard.
L.S. Slevin, photographer.

RIGHT, TOP:

M.E. Church and Dolores Street, looking South, Carmel-by-the-Sea, California.
L.S. Slevin, photographer.
Carmel-by-the-Sea Pharmacy.

RIGHT, BOTTOM:

Ocean Avenue, looking West, Carmel-by-the-Sea, California.
L.S. Slevin, photographer.
Carmel Pharmacy.

M. E. Church and Dolores Street looking South.   Carmel-by-the-Sea, California.

Ocean Avenue, looking West.   Carmel-by-the-Sea, California.

LEFT, TOP:

Ocean Avenue, Carmel by the Sea, California, near Monterey.
J.K. Oliver, photographer.

PICTURESQUE BUSINESS DISTRICT, CARMEL, CALIFORNIA—M 19

LEFT, BOTTOM:

Picturesque Business District, Carmel, California.
C.B. Bender, no. M 19.

HARRISON MEMORIAL LIBRARY
CARMEL, CAL.

L. S. SLEVIN
PHO.

The medley of architectural styles was frequently a postcard subject. In 1924, Hugh G. Comstock built the first fairy-tale cottage to house his wife's considerable doll collection. Comstock was soon inundated with requests to design similar cottages.

On Ocean Avenue and Lincoln Street, the Harrison Memorial Library reflected the California Mission style. Internationally famed architect Bernard Maybeck, a kind-hearted bohemian from Berkeley, provided the design for the free public library. According to Kenneth H. Cardwell, a Maybeck expert and a personal friend of the architect, "Maybeck did not want to do the construction drawings for the library, so he arranged for M.J. Murphy, a contractor builder, to do them. The design drawings were done by Maybeck and he should be the architect of record. Mr. Murphy was supervisor of construction." Attending the opening reception on April 6, 1928, Maybeck remarked, "The new library was created, fundamentally, as the Spanish would have designed it, were they living in our days."

Unfortunately no postcards have yet been found of architect Charles Sumner Greene's own small studio on Lincoln Street, built in 1923. This quiet, modest genius used recycled bricks and wood as building materials and did most of the work himself. His masterpiece, the Dan James Residence in Carmel Highlands, is still worth the trip down the coast; when first completed, its magnificent location perched on a cliff above the sea was a postcard photographer's dream. Later, in 1948, architect Frank Lloyd Wright designed another ocean-front home, a stunning hexagonal stone residence on Carmel Point for Mrs. Clinton Walker.

FACING PAGE:

Harrison Memorial Library, Carmel, California.
L.S. Slevin, photographer.
Pacific Novelty Co., no. 6390.

RIGHT, TOP:

**Picturesque Buildings
Along Ocean Avenue,
Carmel, Calif.**
Bell Magazine Agency, no. M37.

RIGHT, BOTTOM:

**Dolores Street, Carmel,
California.**
V. Williams, photographer.
Publisher unknown.

LEFT, TOP:
Carmel.
Real-photo postcard.
A.C. Heidrick, photographer,
no. 303.

LEFT, BOTTOM:
Untitled.
Real-photo postcard.
Publisher unknown.

Carmel Bath House, Cal.

4177

RIGHT, TOP:

Carmel Bath House, Cal.
Pacific Novelty Co., no. 4177.

RIGHT, BOTTOM:

"Circle of Enchantment,"
California, Carmel by the
Sea, Monterey Peninsula.
[Frank Lloyd Wright House.]
Don Mar Sales Co.

FACING PAGE:

Sunset. Carmel Beach, Cal.
L.S. Slevin, photographer.

Sunset.   CARMEL BEACH, Cal.

©1915 BY
L. S. SLEVIN,

Hand-Colored.

Point Lobos near Pacific Grove, Cal.

On the Point of the Sea Wolves

Traveling south from Carmel to Point Lobos, a distance just under four miles, nineteenth-century visitors would have found the hilly, unpaved road slow going. By horse and buggy the journey might have taken an hour as it passed the turn-off to Carmel Valley, over the Carmel River, then uphill to the most southwestern point of Carmel Bay. Robert Louis Stevenson preferred to walk. While staying in Monterey, he visited Point Lobos in 1879. He was enchanted with the rocky headland, its fissures, hidden coves and beaches. Some Stevenson scholars believe that Point Lobos was his inspiration for *Treasure Island*.

Called *Punta de los lobos marinos* by the Spanish, after the barking of the off-shore sea lions, this spectacular meeting of land and water was occupied by Chinese fishermen and Portuguese whalers as early as 1861. By 1878, developers had their eye on the magnificent site, and a city called Carmelito was planned with 25- and 50-foot lots. Some had already been sold when Alexander MacMillan Allan purchased the 640-acre site in 1898. He bought back the lots and operated an abalone fishing and canning operation in Whaler's Cove with his Japanese partner, Gennosuke Kodani.

The motorcar made Point Lobos more accessible, and it became a favorite location for Hollywood filmmakers, photographers and artists. Chiura Obata, who was already a talented artist when he emigrated from Japan in 1903, felt a deep love for the area; he was a frequent overnight visitor to the Kodani home and painted many watercolor scenes of the surroundings. Louis S. Slevin came with his camera, and his postcards of Point Lobos were very popular, especially his photograph of a still-intact whale skeleton.

FACING PAGE:
Point Lobos near Pacific Grove, Cal.
M. Rieder Publisher, no. 11829.

RIGHT, TOP:

On the Road to Point Lobos from Pacific Grove, Cal.
M. Rieder Publisher, no. 3285.

RIGHT, BOTTOM:

Carmel Valley Scene, California.
Real-photo postcard.
Publisher unknown.

FACING PAGE:

10,000 Abalone Plant, Monterey [unreadable].
[Whaler's Cove, Point Lobos.]
Real-photo postcard.
Publisher unknown, no. 29.

CARMEL VALLEY SCENE, CALIFORNIA.

No. 29 WHALER'S COVE PT. LOBOS

155

Richard Criley recalled his early visits to Point Lobos in his series "Growing Up in the Carmel Highlands," for the *Monterey Herald Weekend Magazine* in 1989:

Point Lobos State Reserve lies just across Gibson Creek's deep canyon from my house. I'm grateful that it will remain in its natural state for my lifetime and far beyond. But I can't help my feelings of nostalgia for Point Lobos as it used to be before it was a park.

The Allans operated the Point as a private picnic ground (admission 50 cents per car). I was about three years old on my first visit [1914]. I still remember my sense of awe when we came upon the giant white whale skeleton which stretched out beside the north shore trail.

The tide pools at Weston Beach—[Edward] Weston had not discovered it yet—were a favorite spot for watching hermit crabs, sea anemones, sea urchins and the infinite variety of living things that adapt their life cycles to the movement of the tides. On occasion, when the tide was low, I harvested mussels and cooked them in a tin can stuffed with seaweed.

I used to think about the native people who for countless centuries had lived in this same spot, watched the same sunsets, gathered the same mussels and abalones. On our side of Gibson Creek they left a midden heap, creating the richest black soil. On Point Lobos, after a rare wind had shifted the sand dunes, I found piles of flint chips where Stone Age artisans shaped their tools and arrowheads.

A.M. Allan died in 1931, and his heirs sold the property to the State of California. The "crown jewel of the State Park System" opened in 1933. Since that time, the Point Lobos State Reserve has added 775 underwater acres surrounding the headland, and additional acreage to protect the Gowen cypress. In 1968, Point Lobos State Reserve became the first registered National Natural Landmark in the California State Park System.

FACING PAGE:

Point Lobos near Y.W.C.A.
Conference Grounds,
Asilomar, Monterey Co.,
Calif.
Cardinell-Vincent Co.

POINT LOBOS NEAR Y.W.C.A. CONFERENCE GROUNDS
ASILOMAR, MONTEREY CO. CALIF.

Devils Caldron Pt. Lobos near Pacific Grove, Cal.

A Rocky Point on the Pacific Coast.

It is very pleasant on the beach.
Anna.

Pt. Lobos near Pacific Grove, Cal.

Dear Grace, The weather has been bad so I couldn't get a picture. I wish you were here.

F. Ordway.

Skeleton of Whale, Point Lobos near Carmel Cal.

Photo by L. S. Slevin, Carmel Cal.

FACING PAGE, FAR LEFT:

Devil's Caldron, Pt. Lobos near Pacific Grove, Cal.
M. Rieder Publisher, no. 11867.

FACING PAGE, TOP:

A Rocky Point on the Pacific Coast.
M. Rieder Publisher, no. 9172.

FACING PAGE, BOTTOM:

Pt. Lobos near Pacific Grove, Cal.
M. Rieder Publisher, no. 11878.

LEFT, TOP:

Skeleton of Whale, Point Lobos near Carmel, Cal.
L.S. Slevin, photographer.

LEFT, BOTTOM:

Untitled.
Real-photo postcard.
Publisher unknown.

RIGHT, TOP:

**"Old Veteran" Cypress,
Point Lobos, Carmel Bay,
California.**
B.W. White, no. 72.

RIGHT, BOTTOM:

**The Old Veteran, Point
Carmel, California.**
The Albertype Co.

FACING PAGE:

**Point Lobos near Pacific
Grove, Cal.**
M. Rieder Publisher, no. 8280.

Point Lobos near Pacific Grove, Cal.

Photo by
L. S. SLEVIN
CARMEL, CAL.

My Home's in the Highlands

The magnificent two miles of coastline just south of Point Lobos, and the high land above it, were first developed in 1916 by Frank Powers and James F. Devendorf. When the Carmel Highlands Inn opened in 1918, there were just a few summer log cabins and one family residence in the settlement. The hill was newly planted with pines, and there were open grassy plots with carpets of wild strawberries. The first residence, an impressive stone house set majestically above Gibson Beach, was owned by the artist Theodore Criley. Photographer Louis Slevin printed postcards of the new Carmel Highlands Inn; Theodore Criley's second son, Richard Criley, refers to one of these postcards in his *Monterey Herald Weekend Magazine* article "Growing Up in the Carmel Highlands":

> Just recently I came across an old postcard advertising the Carmel Highlands Inn, showing a view of the coast barren of any other building. The date is 1918. Along with some practical information like, 'a comfortable auto meets all trains,' there is a P.S.: 'The Highlands is electric lighted. A telephone system is nearly completed.'
>
> Our first couple of years in the Highlands were without any phone nearer than Carmel. Sometime in 1918 or 1919, the Highlands got its 'system,' a single-party line serving the Inn and the growing number of residents, operating on a complex system of signals consisting of combinations of long and short rings. Our number was five short. When the phone rang, we would start counting, trying to distinguish between shorts and longs. If it stopped ringing at less than five, or included long rings, we didn't have to rush to the phone. Since the phone was ringing for much of the day and evening, listening to it occupied a lot of our time.

The Criley home was a bohemian social center. Actors, musicians, artists and poets attended dinners, "fancy dress" dances and theater like "comedia dell'arte" in the large living room facing the sea. The annual Criley Fourth of July party on Gibson Beach was so popular and well-attended that the beach was known for many years as Criley Beach.

FACING PAGE:

A Carmel Highlands Residence, Carmel, California.
[Dan James Residence.]
L.S. Slevin, photographer.
The Albertype Co.

No postcard exists (if it ever did) of the Criley house. But postcards do record two remarkable Highland residences photographed by L.S. Slevin of Carmel: the William Ritschel castle and the Dan James Residence.

The artist William Frederick Ritschel was born in Nuremburg, Germany, in 1864. He began sketching while working on merchant ships and never lost his love of the sea. In 1895, Ritschel emigrated to New York, where his marine paintings were very well-received, and he had many gallery and museum exhibitions. By 1914, he had become a U.S. citizen, and in that year was elected into the National Academy of the Arts, the highest honor given to an American artist. While traveling in the West, he discovered Carmel and decided to settle there. He purchased a bluff above the ocean in 1918, and there he designed and built "Castel a Mare," an unusual, oceanfront house and studio that resembled a castle. The living room–studio had 18-foot walls and large north-facing windows, so he could "live, breathe, eat and paint." Ritschel was a familiar figure in the Highlands, perched on a cliff with easel and brushes; in warm weather he would wear a colorful sarong from one of his South Seas voyages. His fame was international, and during World War II, he melted down all of his gold medals and donated the proceeds to the Red Cross. William Ritschel died at his oceanfront studio-house in 1949.

For five years, from 1918 until 1923, guests of the Carmel Highlands Inn, local residents and visitors watched with curiosity and admiration as the Dan James Residence appeared to grow organically out of a rocky cliff above the sea. Year after year, golden granite of varying thickness was brought by horse cart along the quiet county road from a quarry near Yankee Point. Masonry started forty-five feet down the cliff on a solid purchase of bedrock. Stone walls, two to three feet thick, gradually appeared. The workmanship was so fine that it was difficult to see where the natural rock of the cliff stopped and the walls of the mansion began. Built as a retirement home for the amateur writer and Kansas City retailer Dan James, it was architect Charles Sumner Greene's most creative and ambitious project. The unique arts and crafts masterpiece, situated directly on the cliff below the Carmel Highlands Inn on Highway 1, still draws the attention of students, scholars and the passing tourist.

FACING PAGE:

A Studio, Carmel Highlands, California.
[William Ritschel Castle.]
L.S. Slevin, photographer.
The Albertype Co.

CARMEL HIGHLANDS INN
Carmel, Calif.

SLEVIN
PHOTO

Highlands Inn

CARMEL HIGHLANDS

Four miles South of Carmel on State Highway No. 1

"Where Wintertime Is Summertime!"

The attractive Chalets overlook one of the World's most beautiful seascapes

FACING PAGE:

Carmel Highlands Inn, Carmel, Calif.
L.S. Slevin, photographer.
The Albertype Co.

LEFT, TOP:

Highlands Inn, Carmel Highlands: "Where Wintertime Is Summertime!"
Hotel Informant.

LEFT, BOTTOM:

Lobby, Carmel Highlands Inn, Carmel, California.
The Albertype Co.

RIGHT, TOP:
**A Carmel Highlands
Cottage, Carmel, California.**
L.S. Slevin, photographer.
The Albertype Co.

RIGHT, BOTTOM:
**Carmel Highlands Inn,
Carmel, California.**
L.S. Slevin, photographer.
The Albertype Co.

LEFT, TOP:

Highlands Inn, Carmel, Cal.
L.S. Slevin, photographer.
The Albertype Co.

LEFT, BOTTOM:

**Carmel Highlands Inn,
Carmel, California.**
L.S. Slevin, photographer.
The Albertype Co.

The Long and Winding Road

To those of us who lived on the coast, it was never called Big Sur. It was simply The Coast, as though it were the only coast in the world. It was the Spaniards who labeled it the Sur, *sur* simply being the Spanish word for South. By it they referred to the entire coast lying south of Carmel Mission. Early American settlers identified themselves more precisely in terms of where they lived: Palo Colorado, Garapata, Soberanes Creek, Little Sur, Big Sur, Lucia, etc. Each canyon was different and each had its own history and atmosphere, its *ambiente*. The Big Sur was merely one of these canyons, although it was the biggest one. After the highway went through in 1937, the entire area south of Carmel became known as the Big Sur. Later, to add reinforcement to the place name, avant-garde writer Henry Miller wrote *Big Sur and the Oranges of Hieronymous Bosch*. In the 1950s the Beat writer, Jack Kerouac, came out with a book called *Big Sur*. Its locale was actually Bixby Creek (my old home) and he went down there, ridiculously enough, in a taxi-cab.

—Rosalind Sharpe Wall, *A Wild Coast and Lonely*

The first tourists to venture into this vast and rugged wilderness south of Carmel Highlands came for the hot springs at the north end of what is today Los Padres National Forest. The Tassajara Hot Springs were originally discovered by the Esselen Indians who revered the springs and used them as a traditional ceremonial ground. Vic McGarvey, an early surveyor for Monterey County, was a regular visitor and encouraged others to make the journey. "A Trip to the Hot Springs" by "A Wanderer" was a featured article in the June 24, 1869, *Monterey Gazette*. The article extolled the "healing properties" of the springs and provided a description of a route to get there.

FACING PAGE:

Rocky Shore Line, Carmel–San Simeon Highway, near Big Sur, California.
The Albertype Co.

In 1889, William Hart built a small hotel, a few cabins, a restaurant and a bathhouse. The waters of the springs were reputed to cure everything from rheumatism to neuralgia to stomach ailments. Each summer, more guests arrived.

A paved road to the site was completed by Chinese laborers in 1888, and a larger 40-room sandstone hotel was built by a new owner, Charles Quilty, in 1893. To this remote spot, bowling alley lanes were hauled in for the use of hotel guests. As the bowling alley sections were twenty feet long and the road much narrower and more winding than it is today, it took almost three days to reach the springs.

Hand-tinted color postcards were sold at the hotel, which also must have served as a post office, since some cards carry the postmark "Tassajara Hot Springs."

Robinson Jeffers included the hot springs in his narrative poem "Tamar," and later, during the 1950s, the springs were a popular haunt of Big Sur resident Henry Miller and friends. Today, Tassajara Hot Springs is owned by the San Francisco Zen Center, and guests are welcome during the summer in this still serene and isolated natural setting.

The stage arrives.

TASSAJARA
HOT SPRINGS

Monterey Co.
Calif.

Tassajara Hotel, Tassajara Hot Springs, Monterey Co., Cal.

TASSAJARA HOT SPRINGS, CAL.
JUL 20 P.M. 1918

Miss Eva Paisley
℅ Broderick & Knight
Sausalito
Marin Co
Cal

July 19th 1918

Well Eva Fred & I are having a fine time
Weather very warm Fine Sulphur baths
Good lively crowd This nothing to do but
take baths & eat is great stuff. I ought to
gain about 10 lbs or less Fred & I quit more
the boat on Wednesday morning Hope all Well
J.W.

Two Boiling Springs at Tassajara Hot Springs, Cal.

Natural Mineral Steam Bath over boiling spring at Tassajara Hot Springs.

FACING PAGE, TOP:

Tassajara Hotel,
Tassajara Hot Springs,
Monterey Co., Cal.
M. Rieder Publisher.

FACING PAGE, BOTTOM:

Reverse side of above card.

LEFT, TOP:

Two Boiling Springs at
Tassajara Hot Springs, Cal.
M. Rieder Publisher, no. 57464.

LEFT, BOTTOM:

Natural Mineral Steam Bath
over boiling spring at
Tassajara Hot Springs.
Janssen Litho Co.

RIGHT, TOP:

Trout Stream at Tassajara Hot Springs, Cal.
M. Rieder Publisher, no. 4577.

RIGHT, BOTTOM:

**The Limit,
Tassajara Hot Springs,
Monterey County, Cal.**
M. Rieder Publisher, no. 4579.

FACING PAGE:

**The Narrows,
Tassajara Hot Springs,
Monterey County, Cal.**
M. Rieder Publisher, no. 4578.

OVERLEAF:

**Camping Grounds at
Tassajara Hot Springs,
Monterey County, Cal.**
Publisher unknown.

Trout Stream at Tassajara Hot Springs, Cal.

The Limit, Tassajara Hot Springs, Monterey County, Cal.

The Narrows, Tassajara Hot Springs, Monterey County, Cal.

Camping Grounds at Tassajara. Hot Springs, Monterey County, Cal.

PFEIFFER'S RANCH RESORT.
BIG SUR RIVER, CALIF.

The old county road south from Carmel, narrow and winding with endless switchbacks into every canyon along the coast, ended abruptly at the small community of Big Sur. On steep grades it was just a single-lane road with occasional turnouts for passing. When two cars met, the driver coming downhill was supposed to back uphill to a turnout. Few people ventured down the old road until Florence Swetnam Pfeiffer, wife of pioneer John Pfeiffer, accidentally started the first tourist resort on the coast in 1908.

Florence was an excellent cook, and some visitors took advantage of the Pfeiffers' old-time hospitality of free room and board. In addition to her regular work on the ranch, the extra nonpaying guests meant hauling water, doing the laundry, changing beds and cleaning the rooms. Florence later recalled that historic day when she decided she had had enough:

"A man Mr. Pfeiffer really disliked had stopped at the house to stay all night. He had four of his friends with him and a string of five pack animals. They had their supper, bed and breakfast. Next morning his friends left on the stage without even 'thank you.'" The packer began to abuse one of his mules and in a bold move, Florence told him, "It's your mule and you can beat it, I suppose, but from now on I expect to charge you so much for each horse, so much for each bed, and so much for each meal every time you stop here." Thus began the famed Pfeiffer Ranch Resort, now the site of Big Sur Lodge. "Strange to say," Mrs. Pfeiffer wrote in her journal, "when the people had to pay we had a nicer class of guests who paid cheerfully and continued to come year after year."

FACING PAGE:

**Pfeiffer's Ranch Resort,
Big Sur River, Calif.**
Publisher unknown.

RIGHT, TOP:
Untitled [Big Sur Trail].
Real-photo postcard.
Publisher unknown.

RIGHT, BOTTOM:
Redwood Lodge, Big Sur, Calif.
Real-photo postcard.
Zan of Tamalpais, no. RL3.

HOFFMANS CAMP PALO COLORADO CANYON MONTEREY CALIFORNIA

LEFT, TOP:
Untitled.
Real-photo postcard.
Publisher unknown.

LEFT, BOTTOM:
Hoffmans Camp, Palo Colorado Canyon, Monterey, California.
Publisher unknown.

RAINBOW LODGE PROPERTIES - SHOWING RAINBOW BRIDGE.
15 M. SOUTH OF CARMEL, AND MONTEREY, CALIF.

186

The success of the Pfeiffer Resort encouraged three partners to open a tourist resort in Bixby Canyon, sixteen miles south of Carmel. When their efforts failed, the 300-acre ranch was put up for sale. Retired U.S. Army captain Howard G. Sharpe bought the property in 1919. It was an idyllic, quiet setting to settle down with his wife Frida and infant daughter Rosalind. The 1870 ranch house was surrounded by magnificent mountains, blue-violet with wild lilac, and the canyon was pink with blossoming wild currant. There were singing birds, wild canaries, orange-winged orioles and purple finches. There was a beach nearby and a mile and a half of trout stream, abundant with rainbow trout.

Years later, as a writer for the *Monterey Herald Weekend Magazine*, Rosalind Sharpe Wall recalled the resort their family operated in Bixby Canyon, the opening of the new Coast Highway and the discovery of the "extinct" sea otter in 1938.

[In 1919] my father had great dreams for the place. He renamed it Rainbow Lodge. He put running water in the house, a kitchen sink, and a bathroom with a flush toilet. Curious neighbors came by on horseback to inspect our bathroom which they had never seen before outside the pages of the Montgomery Ward catalogue.

The tourist season at Rainbow Lodge was a short one and all traffic along the coast stopped after Labor Day. "Not a horn was to be heard on the old county road until the following May or June." Construction started on the new Coast Highway in 1929, and Howard Sharpe was paid $4,000 by the State of California for the easement across his property at Bixby Creek.

The hitherto isolated and lonely coast would now be a part of the world. My Father happily used the money to build a place called the Stone House at the northern end of what was to be Bixby Creek Bridge but was called Rainbow Bridge at first, after our resort. Stone House was made from granite hauled up from the beach below and lined with redwood from the Big Creek Mill near Lucia.

By 1932 my father had opened it to the public, as the highway had already been cut that far, leaving the winding old wagon road forever a thing of the past. Now tourists came down to the Stone House and looked at the view from my father's big observation porch.

Alexander J. "Zan" Stark (1890-1967), a successful postcard publisher from Mill Valley, in Marin County, was one of those early visitors. He photographed the coast from Monterey to Big Sur. His postcards of the Stone House at Bixby Creek sold well at the highway dedication ceremony, held in front of the Stone House on July 3, 1937. The ribbon-cutting honors went to Dr. John L.D. Roberts ("Doc Roberts"), one of the initial proponents of a coastal highway; he had started his medical practice as the coast's only doctor and knew from that experience how beautiful, but also how dangerously inaccessible, the region was.

Among the coast's hidden attractions were the southern sea otters, thought to be extinct from over-hunting in the nineteenth century. They had been sighted in a small herd near Point Sur in 1914, but to avoid possible poaching, the sighting was kept secret. All that changed in 1938. Rosalind Sharpe Wall recalls the "rediscovery" by her father Howard Sharpe:

> One day my father saw some peculiar-looking sea animals offshore, playing and floating in the kelp beds as he was gazing through his telescope. He called my mother who got out his binoculars. It occurred to him that they might be sea otters, but how could they be? The southern sea otter had supposedly been extinct for 107 years. In great excitement, he phoned the Hopkins Marine Station....

On May 14, 1938, the *San Francisco Call Bulletin*'s front page headline brought the story to the public's attention. Photographs of the sea otters were accompanied with one of Howard Sharpe and his now-famous telescope. Hundreds of tourists drove down the coast to view sea otters through the telescope at ten cents apiece, while inside, Frida Sharpe sold sandwiches, salad, chili beans... and postcards.

At the County Board of Supervisors in Monterey, Frida Sharpe had spoken eloquently on behalf of preserving the natural beauty of the highway. Today the traveler can appreciate the efforts of Doc Roberts and Frida Sharpe; there are no billboards, no hot dog stands, and no flashy buildings. Instead the journey south along the coast displays some of the most dramatic and unspoiled scenery in the world.

FACING PAGE:

The Rocky Creek Bridge and Pacific Ocean near Rogers Redwood Camp, Big Sur, Calif.
Frashers Fotos.

THE ROCKY CREEK BRIDGE AND
PACIFIC OCEAN NEAR
ROGERS REDWOOD CAMP, BIG SUR, CALIF.

RIGHT, TOP:
Lucia Lodge on Highway No. 1, South of Big Sur, California.
Frashers Fotos, no. F-8306.

RIGHT, BOTTOM:
Point Sur, Carmel – San Simeon Section, California State Highway No. 1.
B.W. White, no. 97.

FACING PAGE:
On the Carmel–San Simeon Highway, California.
The Albertype Co.

Lucia Lodge on Highway No. 1, South of Big Sur, California.   F-8306

97—Point Sur, Carmel-San Simeon Section, California State Highway No. 1

9A-H1965

Index